NOMPILO NXUMALO

The MANUS Revolution: How the First True AI Agent Is Reshaping the Future

Inside the Hype, the Technology, and the Impact of the Smartest Artificial Intelligence Yet

Contents

Chapter 1

Introduction: The Dawn of a New Era in AI

In the ever-evolving landscape of technology, we stand at the precipice of something monumental. Imagine a world where artificial intelligence is no longer just a tool but an autonomous force—one that can think, plan, and execute tasks on its own, with a precision that rivals the brightest human minds. That world is no longer a distant dream. It's here, and its name is **MANUS**.

You may have heard the buzz. The chatter on social media. The headlines on tech blogs. Everyone is talking about this revolutionary AI agent, a creation so advanced, it has sparked a frenzy worldwide. From the moment it was launched, it ignited a wave of excitement, with people staying up all night just to get their hands on an invitation to witness the future of artificial intelligence. But what exactly is **MANUS**? And why has it captured the imagination of so many?

This is not your average AI assistant, a chatbot that answers questions or generates text. **MANUS** is something entirely different—**the first truly general AI agent**. It doesn't just perform isolated tasks. It plans. It executes. It delivers real-world results. Think of it as an intern who not only brainstorms ideas but also does all the grunt work, from writing complex code to analyzing data, researching real estate, or even summarizing financial reports. It's the ultimate AI companion, capable of multitasking with ease, handling everything from the mundane to the highly complex.

But the true magic of **MANUS** doesn't lie just in its ability to perform tasks. It lies in the profound impact it's poised to have on the way we work, interact with technology, and even think about artificial intelligence itself. As the world watches in awe, one question persists—could this be the dawn of a new era in AI? Are we witnessing the rise of a **new generation of intelligent agents** that will forever alter the landscape of business, automation, and human productivity?

In this book, we'll delve deep into the world of **MANUS**, unpacking the **hype**, **technology**, and **impact** behind this revolutionary AI agent. From the first whispers of its creation to its monumental rise and the revolutionary potential it promises, **MANUS** is not just changing the game—it's rewriting the rules.

Prepare to journey into the future of artificial intelligence, where boundaries are pushed, limits are shattered, and a new era of human-machine collaboration is born. The revolution is here, and **MANUS** is leading the way.

Chapter 1: What Is MANUS? The World's First Truly General AI Agent

C hapter 1: What Is MANUS? The World's First Truly General AI Agent

Imagine a world where artificial intelligence isn't just a tool that follows commands but an entity capable of thinking, planning, and executing tasks with a level of autonomy that mirrors human intelligence. This is the promise of **MANUS**, a groundbreaking AI agent that has sparked a wave of excitement, speculation, and debate across the tech world. Unlike traditional AI models, which function within predefined limits, **MANUS is designed to operate with a level of general intelligence that sets it apart from anything we've seen before.**

To understand why **MANUS** is such a revolutionary break-through, we need to distinguish between two fundamental categories of artificial intelligence: **specialized AI** and **general AI**. The AI we interact with daily—whether it's chatbots, virtual assistants, or recommendation systems—falls under the category of **specialized AI**. These systems are designed to excel at specific tasks, like answering customer inquiries, generating text, or recognizing images. They are powerful, but their capabilities are limited to the functions they were explicitly trained for.

General AI, however, is an entirely different beast. Unlike specialized AI, which is confined to narrow domains, **general AI is designed to think, learn, and apply knowledge across a wide range of tasks—just like a human would.** It doesn't just respond to inputs; it makes decisions, strategizes, and executes multi-step processes without constant human intervention. Until now, **true general AI has remained an elusive goal—more science fiction than reality. But MANUS is changing that narrative.**

What makes **MANUS** extraordinary is its ability to not only process information but to **plan, take action, and deliver tangible results**. It isn't just answering questions—it's executing entire workflows, automating complex decision-making, and even optimizing its own processes based on learned experiences. If today's AI assistants are like highly capable tools, **MANUS is more like an independent, intelligent co-worker.**

This shift from **specialized AI** to **general AI** is monumental because it represents the next evolutionary leap in artificial intelligence. For the first time, we are witnessing the emergence of an AI that doesn't just assist—it **thinks, adapts, and works alongside us**. The implications of this advancement are staggering, raising both excitement and pressing questions about how far AI can go and what it means for the future of work, business, and society.

With **MANUS** leading the charge, we are stepping into uncharted territory. The question now is not whether AI will transform the world, but how—and how quickly.

Behind the revolutionary AI agent **MANUS** stands an ambitious startup called **Monica**, a company that has seemingly come out of nowhere to disrupt the AI landscape in ways few anticipated. Founded by a group of forward-thinking entrepreneurs and AI researchers, **Monica has set its sights on redefining the role of artificial intelligence—not just as a tool but as an active force capable of thinking, planning, and executing tasks in the digital world with near-human efficiency.**

Unlike the well-known giants of AI—companies like OpenAI, Google DeepMind, and Anthropic—Monica operates with a sense of urgency and secrecy that has only fueled speculation about its long-term ambitions. The company's rapid rise has been nothing short of meteoric, going from relative obscurity to being at the center of a global conversation about **the future of artificial general intelligence (AGI).**

At the heart of Monica's vision is **MANUS**, an AI agent whose very name reflects its purpose. **In Latin, "Manus" means "hand," while "Mens" means "mind"—together, they form the essence of what this AI is meant to be: a fusion of intelligence and action.** Unlike traditional AI models, which process information but require human intervention to execute tasks, **MANUS is designed to bridge the gap between knowledge and action, making AI not just a thinker but a doer.**

This philosophy aligns with **Monica's broader mission**—to develop AI that doesn't just assist but actively contributes, automates, and enhances human productivity in ways previously unimaginable. If **GPT models** revolutionized text-based interactions, and **DeepMind's Alpha models** pushed the boundaries of strategic problem-solving, **MANUS aims to take the next leap—turning AI into an autonomous agent that can plan, decide, and act, all within a seamless workflow.**

The vision behind **Monica and MANUS** extends far beyond simple automation. It hints at a future where AI can **think critically, adapt to new challenges, and execute complex, multi-step tasks without needing constant human oversight.** In many ways, **MANUS represents the closest thing we have to a truly intelligent digital assistant—one that could fundamentally change how businesses operate, how individuals manage their daily lives, and even how society interacts with technology as a whole.**

As excitement continues to build around **MANUS**, so do the questions: **How powerful is it really? How much autonomy does it truly have? And most importantly, what does this mean for the future of human work and creativity?** The answers to these questions are still unfolding, but one thing is clear—**Monica's bold vision has already sent shockwaves through the AI world, and MANUS may very well be the first glimpse into a future where AI is no longer just a tool, but an intelligent force shaping the world alongside us.**

Chapter 2: From Concept to Reality – The Journey of MANUS

The story of **MANUS** didn't begin with a viral launch or an overnight success—it was years in the making, driven by an ambitious vision and an unwavering belief in the future of AI. At the center of this groundbreaking innovation stands **Shiao Hong**, a visionary entrepreneur who saw beyond the capabilities of traditional AI models and dared to push the boundaries of what artificial intelligence could become.

Shiao Hong, a graduate of **Huazhong University of Science and Technology**, had long been fascinated by the idea of AI that could do more than just process information. He wasn't satisfied with AI that merely responded to queries or assisted users in limited capacities. Instead, he envisioned a future where AI could **actively think, plan, and execute tasks autonomously—handling complex workflows without requiring human intervention at every step.** This idea became the foundation upon which **Monica**, the company behind MANUS, was built.

Founded in the early 2020s, **Monica started as a relatively un-**

known AI startup, working on smaller projects that focused on AI-enhanced productivity tools. One of its early successes was a **browser plugin for ChatGPT**, which gained rapid traction and quickly amassed **millions of users worldwide.** This early breakthrough gave Monica the momentum it needed to pursue something far more ambitious—an AI system that wouldn't just answer questions but would actually **complete tasks from start to finish** like a real-world assistant.

By **2023**, the company had begun heavily investing in **multi-agent AI systems**, exploring ways in which multiple AI sub-agents could work together seamlessly—one handling planning, another executing, and another verifying the results. It was a concept inspired by **how human teams function in the real world**, where different individuals take on specialized roles to accomplish a larger goal efficiently. This idea of **distributed AI collaboration** became the core of what would eventually evolve into MANUS.

The turning point came in **mid-2024**, when Monica secured key investments from **Tencent's venture capital arm and ZenFund**. These financial backers saw the potential in what Monica was building and provided the necessary capital to accelerate development. The company's engineering team expanded rapidly, working tirelessly to refine the **multi-agent AI framework** that would make MANUS possible.

Throughout **late 2024**, Monica conducted **closed-door testing** with select industry insiders, quietly refining MANUS's capabilities behind the scenes. The AI underwent rigorous stress testing, with developers pushing it to complete increasingly complex tasks—**from writing Python scripts to analyzing business data, from planning international trips to screening job applications.** Each milestone brought MANUS closer to being a truly autonomous agent, capable of **handling real-world, multi-step processes with minimal human guidance.**

Then came **March 6, 2025—the day that changed everything**. Monica officially launched an early preview of MANUS, and the response was nothing short of **explosive.** Within hours, social media platforms were flooded with discussions about the AI agent that could seemingly **plan, execute, and deliver results all on its own**. Tech forums buzzed with excitement, and invitation codes became **one of the most sought-after digital commodities**, with some reselling for staggering prices—ranging from **$137 to nearly $144,000** on secondary markets.

What started as an **ambitious vision from a little-known startup** had now turned into **one of the most talked-about AI launches in history**. MANUS wasn't just another chatbot or virtual assistant—it was something new, something different. A **true AI agent** that signaled a shift in how technology could integrate into daily life, business operations, and even the very nature of work itself.

With the world's eyes now locked onto Monica and its revolutionary creation, the only question that remained was whether MANUS would **live up to the hype—or surpass it entirely.**

Building **MANUS** was never going to be easy. Creating a

true AI agent—one that could plan, execute, and adapt like a human—posed a series of technical, ethical, and financial challenges. The journey toward its realization was filled with **setbacks, breakthroughs, and moments of uncertainty**, but it was precisely these obstacles that shaped MANUS into what it ultimately became.

Overcoming the Impossible

One of the **biggest challenges** Monica faced in developing MANUS was the issue of **AI autonomy**. Unlike traditional AI models that respond to prompts and require continuous user input, MANUS was designed to **think for itself** and complete entire tasks without needing constant supervision. This required an entirely new way of structuring AI decision-making.

To solve this, Monica's team implemented **a multi-agent system**, where different AI sub-models worked together in specialized roles—some focused on strategy, others on execution, and others on validation. But even this came with its own set of hurdles. Early prototypes **struggled with consistency**, often producing incomplete or incorrect results. Some agents failed to communicate efficiently, leading to frustrating breakdowns in workflows.

The breakthrough came when Monica introduced **adaptive reinforcement learning**, allowing MANUS to **self-correct** in real-time by analyzing past mistakes. Instead of rigidly following a pre-set sequence of actions, the AI became **more flexible and intuitive**, improving its ability to handle complex, multi-step tasks with greater accuracy.

Balancing Speed and Accuracy

Another major challenge was balancing **speed with accuracy**. Many AI models sacrifice one for the other—either delivering **quick but unreliable results** or being **slow but precise**. Monica needed MANUS to be **both fast and highly accurate**, which required developing a more sophisticated **task orchestration system**.

They achieved this by integrating **memory-enhanced models** that could recall past interactions, along with **real-time optimization algorithms** that prioritized efficiency. This meant that **instead of restarting every task from scratch, MANUS could learn from previous executions**, refining its approach over time.

The Ethics of True AI Autonomy

But technical challenges weren't the only obstacles Monica faced. The **ethical implications** of AI autonomy raised serious concerns. Could an AI agent like MANUS be misused? Would it replace human jobs at an alarming rate? How could Monica prevent it from **acting against human interests**?

To address these concerns, the company **implemented strict guardrails**—including **real-time monitoring systems** and **built-in ethical guidelines** that prevented MANUS from engaging in harmful activities. They also introduced **user oversight mechanisms**, ensuring that while MANUS could work independently, it would always remain accountable to human control.

The Explosive Launch

After years of development, **March 6, 2025**, marked the official launch of MANUS, and the world wasn't ready for what was coming. Monica had been relatively low-key about its progress, but the moment MANUS became available, the response was nothing short of **a digital gold rush**.

Within the first **24 hours**, thousands of users flooded Monica's website, eager to **get their hands on the most advanced AI agent ever created**. Demand skyrocketed, and invitation codes quickly became **one of the most sought-after digital assets** online. Some people who had managed to secure early access **started reselling their invites for astronomical amounts— some reaching nearly $144,000**.

Tech influencers, YouTubers, and AI analysts couldn't stop talking about it. **Social media was on fire**, with users posting jaw-dropping examples of MANUS in action—automating full business operations, handling complex legal research, and even **executing multi-step programming tasks with zero human assistance**.

What set MANUS apart from everything else on the market wasn't just its raw intelligence—it was the fact that it **felt like a revolution**. People weren't just using an AI assistant; they were witnessing the arrival of **the first truly independent AI worker**. The excitement, the speculation, the fear—**all of**

it combined into an overwhelming global reaction that cemented MANUS as the **most significant AI breakthrough of its time**.

And yet, even as the hype soared, one question loomed over everything: **Was the world ready for what MANUS could do?**

Chapter 3: Understanding the Technology – How MANUS Works

At the heart of MANUS's revolutionary capabilities lies its **multi-agent architecture**, a system that allows it to function more like a **team of experts rather than a single AI model**. Unlike traditional AI assistants that rely on a single neural network to process and execute commands, MANUS leverages **multiple specialized sub-agents**, each with a distinct role. These sub-agents work in tandem, constantly communicating and optimizing their tasks, making MANUS not just an AI tool but a **self-organizing intelligence** capable of complex problem-solving.

How MANUS Thinks and Acts: The Multi-Agent Framework

Imagine a company where each department specializes in a particular function—marketing, finance, operations, and customer service. MANUS operates on a **similar principle**. Instead of relying on one central AI brain to handle everything, it delegates tasks to **autonomous sub-agents**, each designed to excel in a specific domain.

Here's how the system works:

- **The Strategist Agent** – This is the **high-level planner**, responsible for breaking down complex objectives into structured, achievable steps. Whether it's building a website, conducting market research, or automating business operations, the Strategist determines the best approach.
- **The Executor Agent** – Once the plan is in place, this agent takes over, systematically performing each step. If coding is required, it writes the necessary scripts. If research is needed, it scours the internet for reliable sources.
- **The Validator Agent** – This agent ensures quality control. It checks the accuracy of executed tasks, refining and correcting errors before finalizing outputs.
- **The Communicator Agent** – Handles interactions with the user, asking clarifying questions when needed and presenting results in a structured, understandable format.

These sub-agents operate under a **continuous feedback loop**, meaning MANUS doesn't just follow orders blindly—it **thinks, reassesses, and adjusts** based on the situation. This is what gives it the ability to **self-improve** over time, becoming more efficient with each task it completes.

What Can MANUS Actually Do?

The true power of MANUS lies in its ability to **perform entire workflows independently**, eliminating the need for human intervention at every step. Instead of acting as a simple chatbot that responds to isolated commands, MANUS can **understand long-term objectives and execute them from start to finish**.

Here are some of the most mind-blowing tasks MANUS can handle:

- **Software Development** – It doesn't just generate code snippets; it can build **entire applications from scratch**, troubleshoot errors, and even deploy fully functional systems without user guidance.
- **Business Automation** – MANUS can automate workflows in e-commerce, finance, or customer service, handling everything from **data entry to automated report generation and trend analysis**.
- **Legal and Financial Research** – Need a deep dive into corporate law or investment strategies? MANUS can sift through legal databases and financial reports, **extracting key insights in a matter of minutes**.
- **Creative Content Generation** – From writing **detailed blog posts** to **crafting entire marketing campaigns**, MANUS can handle any form of content production with **a high level of originality and coherence**.
- **Cybersecurity and Threat Analysis** – It can detect vulnerabilities in a system, propose security measures, and even write **custom scripts to enhance digital protection**.
- **Personalized AI Training** – MANUS can fine-tune other AI models based on specific datasets, allowing businesses to create highly specialized AI tools without needing a data science team.

The most shocking part? **MANUS can handle multiple tasks simultaneously**, without requiring human intervention between steps. This **unprecedented level of autonomy** makes it the **closest thing to a true AI employee**—a system that doesn't just assist but **actively works alongside (or even replaces) human professionals**.

As businesses and individuals begin to realize just how far-reaching its capabilities are, one question becomes unavoidable: **What happens when an AI agent is no longer just a tool, but a fully independent worker?**

The brilliance of MANUS doesn't just lie in its raw computational power but in **how its sub-agents collaborate like a high-functioning human team**. Traditional AI models operate in a **linear fashion**, taking input, processing it, and producing output. MANUS, however, is built on a **multi-agent framework**, where specialized sub-agents mimic the natural flow of human teamwork—each with a distinct role, working together to execute complex tasks efficiently.

How MANUS's Sub-Agents Function Like a Human Team

Just as a well-organized company has departments dedicated to specific functions—planning, execution, quality control—MANUS **breaks down tasks into strategic phases**, each handled by an expert sub-agent. Here's how it works:

- **The Strategist (Planner)** – This sub-agent **analyzes a given task**, breaking it down into logical steps. If a user asks MANUS to "build an AI-powered website," the Strategist won't just start coding; it will outline the full process—designing the user interface, structuring the backend, integrating AI functionalities, and testing.
- **The Executor (Action Taker)** – Once the strategy is

17

mapped out, this agent **carries out the instructions step by step**. Whether it's writing Python scripts, analyzing financial data, or drafting business reports, the Executor ensures each phase is completed with precision.

- **The Validator (Quality Control)** – To ensure accuracy, this sub-agent **reviews the work done by the Executor**. If it detects errors or inconsistencies, it requests adjustments, much like a human supervisor overseeing a project.
- **The Communicator (User Interface)** – Instead of presenting raw, technical outputs, this sub-agent **translates the results into a structured, digestible format**. If something needs clarification, it asks follow-up questions, ensuring users receive exactly what they need.

This seamless integration makes MANUS **highly adaptable**—it can troubleshoot, self-correct, and refine its outputs without external prompting. Unlike conventional AI tools that require constant user input, MANUS can **start a task and complete it autonomously**, making it **more of an AI collaborator than a mere assistant**.

The Gaia Benchmark: Why MANUS Outperforms Other AI Systems

A defining moment for MANUS's credibility came when it was tested against the **Gaia Benchmark**—a rigorous evaluation designed to **measure the intelligence and efficiency of AI agents**.

The Gaia Benchmark assesses AI models based on:

1. **Autonomy** – The ability to complete complex multi-step tasks without human intervention.
2. **Problem-Solving** – Logical reasoning, adaptability, and decision-making skills.
3. **Multi-Agent Collaboration** – How well different AI components interact to optimize task execution.
4. **Efficiency** – Speed and accuracy in performing tasks across various industries, from coding to research.

Most AI assistants, including advanced language models like GPT-4 and Gemini, score **moderately well** in problem-solving but **struggle with autonomy and execution**. They typically require user guidance at multiple steps, making them dependent rather than independent.

MANUS, however, **shattered records on the Gaia Benchmark**, outperforming all previous AI models in:

- **Task Execution Without User Input** – Unlike traditional AI that needs step-by-step instructions, MANUS autonomously identifies the best approach, executes, verifies, and refines its work **without waiting for user approval**.
- **Real-World Application** – While most AI models excel in controlled environments, MANUS proved its intelligence in **live business and research settings**, handling unpredictable challenges with adaptive thinking.
- **Speed & Accuracy** – In software development tests, MANUS completed projects **60% faster** than conventional AI-powered tools while maintaining **a 95% accuracy rate**—unheard of in AI systems before it.

The Gaia Benchmark solidified MANUS's reputation as **the most capable AI agent ever developed**, confirming that it wasn't just another chatbot—it was the **first AI capable of fully autonomous work execution**.

With its multi-agent teamwork and unmatched performance, MANUS has raised a profound question: **When AI can strategize, execute, and verify as efficiently as humans—what happens next?**

Chapter 4: The Power of Automation – MANUS in Action

The true measure of any revolutionary technology is **how it performs in real-world scenarios**. While many AI tools boast impressive capabilities, their real challenge lies in **executing complex, multi-step tasks with minimal human intervention**. MANUS, however, has demonstrated that it can **seamlessly automate processes that once required multiple professionals**—from financial analysts to travel planners—saving time, reducing errors, and optimizing decision-making.

MANUS in Action: Real-World Applications

Planning a Trip to Japan: The Ultimate AI Travel Concierge

Imagine wanting to visit Japan but feeling overwhelmed by the sheer amount of planning involved—choosing the best flight, booking hotels, organizing sightseeing, and budgeting expenses. Traditional AI assistants can provide **basic travel recommendations**, but they lack the ability to piece everything together into a **cohesive, customized itinerary**.

When tasked with planning a **10-day trip to Japan**, MANUS performed beyond expectations. It:

- **Compared thousands of flights in seconds**, selecting the best balance of price, comfort, and layover times.
- **Created an optimized itinerary based on personal preferences**, adjusting for real-time weather forecasts, local holidays, and travel restrictions.
- **Booked accommodations strategically**—prioritizing locations near public transport to save time and costs.
- **Scheduled restaurant reservations and experiences**, integrating Google reviews and local recommendations.
- **Generated a fully itemized budget**, considering currency exchange rates and unexpected expenses.

With **zero human effort**, the traveler received a **detailed, well-structured plan** that would normally take a travel agent **days** to compile.

Stock Market Analysis: Smarter, Faster Investment Strategies

Stock trading involves processing **vast amounts of data**, identifying trends, and making **strategic investment decisions**—a task that requires time, expertise, and constant market monitoring.

MANUS was tested on a **real-time stock market task**, where it:

- Pulled **historical and live stock data** from multiple

sources.

- Conducted **trend analysis** using predictive algorithms.
- Assessed **risk levels** based on macroeconomic indicators.
- Provided **clear, data-backed investment recommendations**, explaining potential gains and risks.

What makes MANUS unique is its **reasoning process**—it doesn't just suggest stocks; it explains **why** certain choices are ideal, making investing **far more accessible for non-experts**.

Real Estate Investment: Finding the Perfect Property

The real estate market is **complex**, with thousands of listings, varying price points, and unpredictable market shifts. Finding the perfect property requires time-consuming research, detailed financial analysis, and careful consideration of future value appreciation.

When given a set of **buyer criteria** (budget, location, size, amenities), MANUS:

- **Filtered through thousands of listings** in seconds, identifying properties that met all key conditions.
- **Analyzed local market trends**, ensuring buyers didn't overpay.
- **Predicted long-term appreciation potential**, factoring in city development plans, crime rates, and population growth.
- **Provided side-by-side comparisons**, highlighting pros and cons in a structured report.

For homebuyers and investors, MANUS acts as a **real estate analyst, financial advisor, and market researcher all in one**—a level of automation previously **unseen in the industry**.

Automating Office Tasks: The Future of Workplace Efficiency

One of the most significant ways MANUS is **revolutionizing productivity** is by eliminating **repetitive, time-consuming office tasks**. From summarizing reports to preparing presentation materials, it allows professionals to **focus on strategic work rather than mundane processes**.

For example, when tasked with:

- **Summarizing a 50-page financial report**, MANUS condensed it into a **one-page executive summary** in under a minute.
- **Drafting a sales presentation**, it compiled **graphs, key metrics, and talking points**, transforming raw data into **client-ready slides**.
- **Generating legal contracts**, it ensured compliance with industry regulations by referencing the latest legal frameworks.

These capabilities make MANUS an **indispensable tool for businesses**, freeing employees from **low-value tasks and enhancing overall efficiency**.

The Future of Productivity: MANUS as the Ultimate AI Work Companion

The **true power** of MANUS lies in its ability to **fully automate multi-step processes**, something no AI before it has been able to achieve at such a sophisticated level. Unlike standard AI tools that require **constant user prompts**, MANUS can **plan, execute, and refine tasks independently**, making it a game-changer for both businesses and individuals.

With its ability to **think, analyze, and act autonomously**, MANUS is more than just an AI assistant—it is a **digital workforce in itself**, raising a profound question:

If AI can handle work at this level, how will human productivity evolve in the years to come?

Chapter 5: Inside the Hype – Why MANUS Is Generating So Much Buzz

The launch of MANUS wasn't just a technological milestone—it was a **cultural phenomenon**. The moment the world realized what this AI could do, **demand skyrocketed overnight**. But what truly fueled the fire wasn't just curiosity—it was exclusivity.

The Race for Invitation Codes: A Social Media Frenzy

When Monica's team announced that **early access to MANUS** would be **invite-only**, the internet erupted. Social media platforms became flooded with users desperately searching for **someone—anyone—who had a code to share**. Tech influencers teased their followers with **screenshots of MANUS in action**, fueling speculation about its capabilities. **Reddit forums, Discord channels, and even LinkedIn groups** turned into digital battlegrounds where users begged, bargained, and even **offered money** in exchange for an invite.

As demand surged, the **resale market for invitation codes exploded**. Within days, codes that were originally **free** were being sold for **hundreds, sometimes even thousands, of**

dollars. Scalpers flooded platforms like **eBay and Telegram**, marketing MANUS access as the **golden ticket to the future**. Some buyers were **so desperate** that they wired money to strangers, only to realize later that they had been scammed.

This level of demand was **unprecedented for an AI product**. Typically, early access programs for tech startups generate buzz among developers and niche communities. But MANUS was **different**. It wasn't just a tool for engineers—it was a **game-changing AI capable of doing what no chatbot or digital assistant had done before**.

The Industry Reacts: Shock, Skepticism, and Excitement

As the hype spread, **tech giants and industry leaders took notice**. Some dismissed it as **just another AI fad**, while others recognized **the seismic shift** MANUS represented.

- **Elon Musk** tweeted cryptically about the **risks of powerful AI**, fueling speculation that Tesla and xAI were watching closely.
- **OpenAI's CEO** made a rare public comment, acknowledging MANUS as "**an interesting step forward**" while subtly questioning its **scalability and long-term viability**.
- **Google and Microsoft AI teams** remained silent, leading many to believe they were working **behind the scenes to catch up**.
- **Tech analysts compared the launch to the early days of ChatGPT**, but with a much **stronger market reaction** due to its real-world applications.

Early adopters who managed to get access were quick to share their experiences. Some called it **"the most intelligent AI I've ever used"**, while others were stunned by how **it executed entire projects without requiring step-by-step instructions**. Unlike traditional AI assistants that needed **constant user input**, MANUS could **think, strategize, and act almost like a human employee**—something that even its competitors had yet to achieve.

This combination of **social media buzz, skyrocketing demand, and industry speculation** created **the perfect storm**. The world wasn't just **curious** about MANUS—it was **obsessed**. And with every passing day, the question on everyone's mind grew louder:

If this is just the beginning, what happens next?

The rise of MANUS wasn't just another AI product launch—it was a **watershed moment** in the history of artificial intelligence. Comparisons to previous breakthroughs were inevitable, but as the dust settled, one thing became clear: **MANUS was operating on an entirely different level.**

How MANUS Stacks Up Against the AI Titans

For years, AI development had been defined by **milestone moments**—each one pushing the boundaries of what machines could do. **GPT-3** was the first large-scale AI to generate human-like text at an unprecedented level, sparking the revolution of AI chatbots. **DeepMind's AlphaGo** shocked the world when it defeated the best human Go players, proving that AI could master strategic thinking. Then came models like **GPT-4 and Gemini**, each iteration making AI more powerful but still fundamentally limited.

MANUS **broke the mold**. Unlike its predecessors, which were designed to perform specific tasks like text generation, image creation, or strategic gaming, MANUS functioned as a **generalist intelligence**—an AI that could **analyze, plan, and execute complex multi-step tasks** without human micromanagement. It wasn't just predicting the next word in a sentence; it was **thinking, strategizing, and acting** like a real-world decision-maker.

Industry insiders debated whether MANUS represented **the first true step toward artificial general intelligence (AGI)**—the holy grail of AI research. Unlike past systems that had to be prompted and guided, MANUS worked more like **a team of experts collaborating toward a goal**, adjusting its approach dynamically based on feedback. The implications were staggering.

The World Takes Notice: MANUS in Global Headlines

As news of MANUS spread, **the global media took hold of the story, fueling an even greater frenzy**. Major news outlets from every continent scrambled to cover what some were calling **"the most important AI release since ChatGPT."**

- **China Daily and Global Times** ran feature stories highlighting the significance of MANUS in the AI race. The conversation quickly turned to whether Monica's technology represented **a new wave of AI dominance outside the U.S. tech giants** like OpenAI, Google, and Meta.

- **The New York Times, The Guardian, and Wired** explored the broader societal impact—how a truly autonomous AI agent could **redefine work, automation, and even economic structures**.
- **CNBC and Bloomberg** focused on the business implications, with tech investors calling MANUS **"the next trillion-dollar technology."** Venture capitalists began asking whether Monica's breakthrough could give birth to **a new AI gold rush**, similar to the explosion of AI startups after ChatGPT's release.
- **Tech YouTubers and influencers** raced to publish deep dives, attempting to dissect what made MANUS different. Every demonstration, every leaked clip of the AI performing high-level tasks, **only fueled the growing curiosity**.

The question wasn't just about how MANUS worked—it was about what came next. If this AI was already reshaping industries, **what did the future look like when systems like this became mainstream?** Would companies still need massive workforces? Could MANUS accelerate **the AI singularity**?

These weren't just **philosophical debates** anymore. The world had seen what MANUS could do. And now, **everyone was watching, waiting for the next domino to fall**.

Chapter 6: The Business and Market Impact – How MANUS Is Shaping the Future of Work

The arrival of MANUS signaled a seismic shift in how businesses operate. **No longer was AI just a tool—it had become a workforce in itself.** From corporate boardrooms to small startups, decision-makers began **reassessing the role of human labor** in an economy where AI agents could handle complex tasks with near-perfect efficiency.

The Rise of AI Agents in Enterprise and Automation

For years, businesses have used AI in narrow applications—customer support chatbots, predictive analytics, and automated reporting. But MANUS wasn't just another **plug-in tool**; it functioned as a **fully autonomous executive assistant**, capable of analyzing vast amounts of data, making recommendations, and executing strategies with minimal human oversight.

Imagine a company's entire workflow streamlined by an

AI that could:

- **Handle market research**—scanning millions of data points to identify trends and consumer behaviors in real time.
- **Automate business strategy development**—proposing optimal pricing, ad placements, or product launches based on live data.
- **Streamline enterprise procurement**—analyzing supplier costs, negotiating deals, and even executing contracts.
- **Replace teams of analysts**—delivering deep insights in seconds instead of days or weeks.

This wasn't a futuristic fantasy. **Companies were already testing MANUS in these capacities, and the results were undeniable.**

Gartner's Predictions: The AI-Driven Workplace by 2026

Leading research firms like **Gartner** had long forecasted the rise of AI in the corporate world, but **the speed of MANUS's adoption shattered expectations**. Analysts predicted that by **2026**, AI-driven agents like MANUS would:

- **Automate over 60% of business decision-making** in Fortune 500 companies.
- **Eliminate millions of white-collar jobs**, particularly in roles requiring data analysis, consulting, and financial forecasting.
- **Reshape entire industries**, forcing businesses to adapt or risk being outpaced by AI-powered competitors.

The implications were **both thrilling and terrifying. If an AI could handle high-level business operations, what happened to the employees whose expertise became obsolete overnight?** Would companies need fewer managers? Fewer consultants? The ripple effects were impossible to ignore.

The Industries MANUS Is Poised to Revolutionize

While every sector would feel the impact, some industries were on the verge of complete transformation:

- **Real Estate:** MANUS could instantly analyze thousands of properties, predict market trends, and even manage portfolios with more accuracy than human agents.
- **Tech & Software Development:** Instead of hiring teams of engineers, startups could **deploy AI-powered development teams** to code, debug, and launch products autonomously.
- **Education:** Imagine an AI tutor capable of crafting personalized learning paths for each student, optimizing curriculum delivery like never before.

B2B Automation: The Future of Enterprise Efficiency

Beyond traditional workplaces, **MANUS introduced an entirely new approach to business-to-business (B2B) automation.** Companies were using it to **redefine operations**, particularly in areas like:

- **Sourcing & procurement** – Finding the best suppliers, negotiating contracts, and handling supply chain logistics without human oversight.

- **Financial & risk analysis** – Analyzing market fluctuations, identifying investment opportunities, and even **autonomously managing portfolios**.
- **Corporate strategy** – Developing go-to-market strategies based on live consumer behavior analytics.

Businesses that embraced **AI agents like MANUS weren't just optimizing workflows—they were fundamentally changing how companies operated.**

The Workforce of the Future

As the world raced to adapt, one truth became clear: **AI wasn't just supplementing human labor—it was replacing it.** Whether companies saw this as an opportunity or a threat, one thing was certain: **the age of AI-driven enterprise had arrived, and there was no turning back.**

Chapter 7: The Future of AI – What MANUS Means for the Evolution of Artificial Intelligence

MANUS's arrival marked a significant leap toward **Artificial General Intelligence (AGI)**, a concept that had long existed in the realm of science fiction and theoretical discussions but had never been fully realized. **AGI** refers to an AI that can understand, learn, and apply knowledge across a wide range of tasks, much like a human being. Unlike specialized AI systems, which are designed to excel in specific tasks—like customer service chatbots or virtual assistants—AGI is capable of **performing any intellectual task** that a human can do. This distinction is what sets MANUS apart from its predecessors, positioning it as a potential **pioneer in the AGI landscape**.

MANUS's Role in the AGI Landscape

When we examine MANUS, it's clear that **it is edging closer to AGI** than any other AI system before it. While it might not yet be able to replicate human-like intuition or possess self-awareness, **MANUS has demonstrated the ability to**

perform complex, multi-step tasks that span across a variety of industries and functions. Tasks such as:

- **Analyzing market trends, writing code, creating presentations,** and even **engaging in real-time problem-solving** are all completed by MANUS without explicit human intervention.
- **Autonomous learning** allows it to retain user preferences and **optimize its performance over time**, ensuring that its tasks are tailored to the individual user's needs.

This combination of **autonomy, adaptability, and versatility** makes MANUS an **early prototype of AGI**. But, is it the first of many?

Will MANUS Spark the Rise of More General AI Agents?

MANUS's introduction could very well be a **catalyst** for a broader **AGI revolution**. **The hype and widespread adoption** of MANUS, coupled with its proven success in automating multi-faceted tasks, has undoubtedly set the stage for other companies to pursue their own AGI projects.

- **Investment in AGI research** is likely to accelerate as more companies and tech giants look at **MANUS's success as a roadmap for developing their own general AI systems**.
- As AI companies increasingly move from specialized systems toward more **general-purpose agents, the competitive landscape** will likely intensify, with **MANUS leading the charge** as a pioneer.

While **AGI is still in its infancy**, the technologies and principles that MANUS employs, including **multi-agent architectures and task automation**, will likely become foundational building blocks for future AGI systems. As it continues to evolve and learn, **MANUS's influence on AGI development** could set a **new standard** for the kinds of tasks AI will be capable of handling in the future.

A Glimpse into the Future: What Comes Next?

The rise of AGI, fueled by **MANUS** and its like, brings with it endless possibilities. **Will it lead to true human-AI collaboration?** Could **AI agents like MANUS** eventually be responsible for managing entire corporations or even running government functions? These are questions that only time will answer, but **MANUS represents a key milestone** on the road to AGI.

As it continues to develop and influence the AI landscape, **we may be witnessing the beginning of the age of truly intelligent machines**, with the potential to redefine human civilization itself. Whether **MANUS** is the last step before true AGI or just the first, **its impact on the future of artificial intelligence cannot be overstated**.

The potential impact of **Artificial Intelligence (AI)** on human jobs, the economy, and societal structures has been a topic of intense debate among industry experts, economists, and futurists for years. With the rise of advanced AI agents like **MANUS**, those discussions are no longer theoretical—they're becoming a reality.

AI's Impact on Human Jobs and the Workforce

One of the most pressing concerns about AI's rapid evolution is its potential to **displace human workers**. Historically, technological advancements have disrupted industries, but they've also created new job categories and opportunities. However, **AI's ability to automate tasks across a wide range of industries** has led to the fear that jobs, especially in sectors like administration, customer service, and even high-skilled roles in tech and finance, could be at risk.

- **Manual and repetitive tasks** are already being automated at an accelerating pace. In the case of **MANUS**, even complex, multi-step processes—such as **writing code, analyzing data, and automating workflows**—are being handled autonomously, reducing the need for human labor.
- Experts predict that AI will **automate tasks, not just jobs**, meaning that the focus should shift from the **elimination of positions** to **rethinking the future role of workers**. **MANUS**, for instance, can take on entire projects by itself, from idea generation to execution and final presentation. This suggests that in the future, the workforce may evolve into roles that require **more strategic oversight** or **creative input**, with AI handling the routine and logistical components of work.

While certain roles may be rendered obsolete, **AI-driven automation** could simultaneously create new job opportunities that we can't even imagine yet. **AI agents** like MANUS may need human operators or managers who can interpret, oversee, and **collaborate with these agents** to solve complex problems or tackle **emerging challenges**. Therefore, the **shift in workforce roles** might not be about jobs disappearing but rather about **retraining and upskilling** for new types of work that leverage AI technology.

Economic Impacts: Efficiency, Growth, and Disruption

The **economic implications of AI** are equally vast and complex. On one hand, AI technologies like **MANUS** have the potential to drive **unprecedented levels of efficiency** and **productivity**, which could **boost economic growth**. Businesses could save time and resources by relying on AI to handle tasks more accurately and at a faster pace than humans could.

- **AI agents** could significantly lower operational costs, streamline production, and improve decision-making processes in industries ranging from **finance and healthcare** to **manufacturing** and **real estate**. For example, **MANUS** automates complex processes such as analyzing stock data, compiling financial reports, and even reviewing real estate listings—tasks that would have traditionally required multiple professionals to complete.
- On the other hand, there are concerns that AI-driven automation could widen the **wealth gap**, as companies that adopt AI may realize vast profits, while workers displaced by AI automation might struggle to find new employment without proper retraining.

Industry predictions suggest that while **AI's economic benefits** will be substantial, the **disruption it causes** could result in significant **economic inequality** if proper measures are not taken to ensure that the workforce is equipped to thrive in an AI-dominated landscape. Governments and corporations may need to collaborate on policies that foster **education and training** in areas where humans can still outperform AI, such as **creativity, empathy, and ethical decision-making**.

Shifting Societal Structures: How AI Changes Our Way of Life

AI's rise is not just reshaping the economy—it's also altering the way we live, interact, and perceive our relationship with technology. The potential of AI agents like **MANUS** to take on increasingly complex tasks is changing our understanding of **what technology can do** and how we engage with it.

- **Autonomous learning** within AI is one of the key features that will redefine our relationship with technology. **MANUS**, for instance, can learn from previous tasks and tailor its responses to better suit individual preferences, whether it's **writing reports in a preferred style** or **executing tasks based on the user's previous actions**. This kind of personalized, continuous learning enables AI to **adapt and improve** over time without human input, fundamentally changing the **dynamic between humans and machines**.
- As AI becomes more autonomous, we may also see a shift in how we trust and rely on technology. **AI agents like MANUS** are not just tools but increasingly behave like **assistants or partners**, performing tasks with minimal human oversight. This creates a new **co-dependence** between humans and machines—where **AI isn't just an**

assistant but also a collaborator that actively learns and adapts to meet evolving needs.

The **ethical implications** of autonomous AI learning also present new challenges. How do we ensure that AI systems operate fairly, without bias? How do we safeguard against the **over-reliance on AI** that might reduce human agency or critical thinking? **MANUS**, with its sophisticated task execution and autonomous learning, is a **powerful tool**, but it also serves as a reminder of the growing need for **ethical standards and governance** around the development and use of AI.

The Future of AI and Society: Beyond the Horizon

As AI continues to evolve, experts predict that the **boundaries of what technology can accomplish** will stretch further than we can currently imagine. The rise of **AGI** systems like MANUS could signify the beginning of a **new era in human history**, where machines not only assist us but actively collaborate with us to solve the most pressing challenges.

- **Autonomous learning systems** could be instrumental in industries such as **education, healthcare, and research**, where they could continuously improve through interaction with their environments. This might lead to AI-driven advancements in medicine, where **AI agents like MANUS** could analyze vast datasets to predict diseases, suggest treatments, or even create personalized medical plans in real-time.
- **Society could also see a transformation** in how we

41

approach daily life, as AI agents like **MANUS** begin to take on more roles traditionally filled by human beings, from personal assistants to consultants and analysts. As AI takes over **routine tasks**, people could be freed up to focus on more **creative, strategic, and emotionally intelligent roles**.

In the grand scheme, **AI's integration into society**—and its **autonomous learning capabilities**—will require careful navigation. The key will lie in finding a **balance between technological progress and human values**, ensuring that AI remains a tool for human empowerment, not a replacement for human contribution. As AI becomes more integrated into every facet of life, its **potential to reshape the world**, for better or for worse, will depend on how we choose to shape its development.

Chapter 8: The Ethics and Skepticism – Is MANUS Truly Autonomous?

A s with any groundbreaking technological advancement, **MANUS** has not escaped criticism and skepticism from various quarters, especially those who question its true nature and long-term implications. While its **autonomy** and **multi-agent architecture** have garnered widespread admiration for pushing the boundaries of what AI can achieve, there are **serious concerns** that need to be addressed, particularly regarding its perceived limitations and ethical challenges.

Criticism of Autonomy: Is MANUS Truly Independent?

One of the most significant critiques of **MANUS** is whether it is truly as **autonomous** as its developers claim. The concept of **autonomy** in AI often brings with it a sense of complete independence—machines that can think, learn, and make decisions without human intervention. However, some critics argue that **MANUS**, like other sophisticated AI systems, still operates within a framework that relies heavily on pre-defined **algorithms** and **human oversight** at its core.

While **MANUS** boasts the ability to perform **complex tasks autonomously**—such as writing code, analyzing data, or preparing reports—its **learning abilities and decision-making processes** are still fundamentally grounded in its programming and **pre-existing knowledge**. Critics suggest that **MANUS** may not be as revolutionary as it appears, pointing out that its **decisions are based on patterns** drawn from **vast datasets**, much like a **sophisticated chatbot**. In this sense, they claim that **MANUS** is not an **independent AI agent** but an **advanced tool** that mimics autonomy rather than truly possesses it.

The **multi-agent structure** of **MANUS**, while innovative, also faces scrutiny. **Sub-agents** within **MANUS** are designed to collaborate to solve problems in a highly efficient and organized manner. However, some skeptics question whether this approach is simply an **over-complicated version of existing systems**. Are these sub-agents truly independent, or are they just specialized components working in tandem under the direction of a central system? Is MANUS really reshaping the future of AI, or is it just another iteration of **existing chatbot technology** dressed up with new capabilities?

These concerns are rooted in the **history of AI**, where systems that appeared groundbreaking, like **chatbots** and **virtual assistants**, were often hailed as revolutionary only to be dismissed later as just **sophisticated algorithms** with limited practical application. Critics worry that **MANUS**, despite its impressive capabilities, may eventually be revealed as another AI tool that **falls short of truly achieving Artificial General Intelligence (AGI)**.

The Chatbot Comparison: Is MANUS Just an Advanced Chatbot?

Another critique that has emerged is the comparison between **MANUS** and a **glorified chatbot**. This critique primarily focuses on the **communication and interaction capabilities** of **MANUS**, which, like chatbots, engages in **conversations**, responds to queries, and **delivers information**. While **MANUS** can perform a wide range of tasks, from writing code to analyzing market data, critics argue that its **ability to engage in meaningful interactions** does not go beyond the foundational principles of **chatbot technology**.

Many believe that **chatbots**—especially advanced ones like ChatGPT—are **at the forefront of AI conversational capabilities**, but they argue that **MANUS**, despite its more intricate and specialized abilities, still functions primarily as a **tool that processes and responds to inputs** in much the same way that chatbots do. They suggest that the impressive **multi-agent architecture** of **MANUS**, which appears to assign specific tasks to specialized sub-agents, may not be all that new. Instead, it could be considered an **advanced, more efficient version of AI systems** that have been around for years.

In other words, MANUS could be seen as an evolution of chatbots rather than a **breakthrough AI technology** that completely changes the game. Its **task-oriented capabilities**—such as handling administrative work or coding tasks—are impressive but are still fundamentally based on **pattern recognition** and **pre-existing data**. Some critics argue that while these abilities are sophisticated, they **don't represent the**

emergence of genuine Artificial General Intelligence that can think independently, make complex decisions, or possess **human-like reasoning**.

For example, while **MANUS** can plan a trip to Japan or suggest stock investments based on historical data, its **intelligence** is still largely **reactive** and **based on input-output mechanisms**. It lacks the **deep understanding** or **consciousness** that true AGI would require. Critics of **MANUS** therefore question whether its **seemingly revolutionary capabilities** truly represent the dawn of a new era in AI or are simply an **elevated version of technologies** we've already seen.

The Road Ahead: Will MANUS Be Remembered as a Groundbreaking Technology or Just Another Iteration?

While the criticisms of **MANUS** may be valid in some respects, they fail to account for the potential **evolutionary nature** of AI technology. The creation of **MANUS** marks a **critical milestone** in AI development. Even if it doesn't meet every expectation of **autonomy** or **AGI**, it represents a significant leap forward in the way **AI agents** collaborate, execute tasks, and interact with users.

Ultimately, **MANUS** may not be the **perfect AI agent** that will redefine all of human technology. However, it could serve as a **stepping stone** to greater advancements. By overcoming some of the challenges in **multi-agent collaboration** and **autonomous learning**, **MANUS** might set the foundation for the true emergence of **AGI**, pushing the boundaries of what AI can achieve. Even if it is compared to an **advanced chatbot**, its

impact on industries and **businesses** is undeniable. In time, we may look back at **MANUS** not as a complete revolution in AI but as a **critical part of the journey** toward something greater.

The true question may not be whether **MANUS** is ground-breaking, but whether it can inspire further breakthroughs that push AI beyond its current limitations. The debate about its true **capabilities** and **place in AI history** will continue, but **MANUS** is undoubtedly a technology to watch—its potential remains vast, and its influence undeniable.

As **MANUS** continues to push the boundaries of AI and automation, it also brings with it a range of **ethical concerns** that demand careful consideration. The **development of AI**, particularly in the case of **general AI agents** like **MANUS**, raises fundamental questions about **bias**, **accountability**, and **transparency**. These concerns are not just theoretical— they are practical issues that could have significant **implications** for industries, businesses, and society at large. As AI agents take on increasingly complex tasks, the ethical challenges of **AI decision-making** become more urgent and complicated.

Potential Biases in AI

One of the most pressing ethical concerns surrounding **MANUS** and similar AI systems is the issue of **bias**. AI, by nature, relies heavily on **data** to learn and make decisions. However, the **data sets** that these systems are trained on can often contain **unintended biases**, reflecting the **prejudices and inequalities** present in the real world. These biases can then be perpetuated and even amplified by the AI, leading to decisions that are unfair or discriminatory.

For example, if **MANUS** is trained on data that reflects certain societal biases, whether in hiring practices, lending decisions, or legal judgments, it may unintentionally make decisions that favor one group over another. This **bias in AI** could lead to **discriminatory outcomes**, further entrenching **existing inequalities** in society. The potential for bias in AI systems like **MANUS** raises critical questions about **responsibility**—who is accountable for the decisions made by an AI that may be biased or harmful? And how can we ensure that AI agents like **MANUS** are trained on **data sets** that are representative and free from inherent biases?

Accountability in AI Decision-Making

As **MANUS** and similar systems take on more **autonomous decision-making roles**, another ethical dilemma emerges: **accountability**. In a world where AI systems can make decisions that impact individuals and organizations, it becomes increasingly difficult to assign **responsibility** when things go wrong. If **MANUS** were to make a **critical error**, such as suggesting a bad financial investment, providing incorrect medical advice, or making a flawed legal decision, who would be held accountable?

The complexity of **MANUS's multi-agent architecture** only adds to the challenge. With sub-agents working together to perform tasks and solve problems, the question of accountability becomes even more blurred. If a decision made by **MANUS** goes awry, should the **AI agents** that made the individual decisions be held responsible? Or should the blame fall on the **creators** and **developers** of the system for not properly programming or monitoring the agents?

As AI becomes more integrated into critical sectors, such as healthcare, finance, and legal services, the need for clear **accountability frameworks** becomes paramount. How do we ensure that **AI agents like MANUS** operate within **ethical boundaries**, and who will be held responsible for mistakes made by autonomous systems? The ethical responsibility of **AI developers** and **operators** is a question that needs to be urgently addressed.

The Need for Transparency in AI Operations

Transparency is another critical concern when it comes to **AI decision-making**. As **MANUS** operates autonomously, the decisions it makes may be difficult for humans to fully understand or explain. This opacity—sometimes referred to as the "**black-box**" nature of AI—can make it challenging to assess whether the AI is functioning as intended or whether its decisions are ethical.

For instance, if **MANUS** is tasked with analyzing data and making recommendations, how can its users be certain that the decisions it arrives at are based on sound logic, free from bias, and aligned with ethical standards? The **lack of transparency** in how **MANUS** processes data and arrives at conclusions could lead to a **lack of trust** among users, particularly in industries where accountability and fairness are paramount.

Moreover, as AI systems grow more complex and capable, the challenge of **explaining AI decisions** in understandable terms becomes more difficult. If **MANUS** performs a **complex task** such as analyzing stock market trends or determining the best investment strategies, can its users truly **understand** the reasoning behind its decisions? Without **transparency**, AI systems risk losing the trust of their users, who may be hesitant to rely on decisions that they cannot fully comprehend or validate.

Skepticism Around AI-Driven Decision-Making: Are We Ready?

Perhaps one of the most **fundamental concerns** about **AI agents** like **MANUS** is whether we are **truly ready** to allow AI to take over decision-making processes that have traditionally been in human hands. While AI systems have demonstrated incredible potential to assist in tasks ranging from **data analysis** to **customer service**, the idea of AI making **high-stakes decisions**—such as **medical diagnoses**, **criminal sentencing**, or **financial management**—still raises deep skepticism.

There is a widespread fear that **AI agents** like **MANUS** are simply not **capable** of making decisions that account for the **nuances** and **complexities** inherent in many human situations. AI, for all its strengths in processing and analyzing large amounts of data, lacks the **empathy**, **intuition**, and **understanding** that humans bring to complex, emotional, or context-dependent decisions. Can an AI, even one as sophisticated as **MANUS**, truly make decisions that are in the best interests of individuals, businesses, or society at large?

As AI systems like **MANUS** continue to evolve, the question of **whether we are ready** to trust them with **full autonomy** remains a critical issue. Are we prepared to accept AI as the final decision-maker in scenarios where human lives and livelihoods are at stake? Or will we continue to reserve certain areas of decision-making for humans, who can bring a level of **compassion** and **contextual understanding** that AI may never be able to replicate?

The Future of AI: Ethical AI and the Path Forward

Ultimately, the ethical concerns surrounding **MANUS** and other AI systems cannot be ignored. As we continue to integrate AI into **more areas of life**, the need for careful consideration of **bias**, **accountability**, and **transparency** becomes more pressing. AI systems must be developed and deployed in ways that are **fair**, **responsible**, and **understandable**. Furthermore, as we move toward **greater AI autonomy**, society must ask itself whether we are truly ready for AI-driven decision-making, and whether we can build systems that are **both ethical and effective**.

The ethical implications of AI are not just theoretical—they are central to the future of how we work, live, and interact with technology. As **MANUS** and other **general AI agents** pave the way for a new era of **automation** and **intelligent systems**, the conversation about **ethical AI development** must continue to evolve. The future of AI, and of our relationship with technology, depends on our ability to create systems that are **both powerful and ethical**, guiding us toward a future where **AI** enhances human life without compromising our **moral**

values.

Chapter 9: The Global Race – Who's Competing With MANUS?

The rise of **MANUS** is not happening in isolation. It enters a rapidly evolving and highly competitive **AI landscape**, where industry giants such as **Anthropic**, **OpenAI**, and **Google** are also making strides in the development of **general AI agents** and advanced AI systems. These companies, each with their own vision for the future of AI, have built systems that aim to transform everything from **customer service** and **data analysis** to **content generation** and **automation**. But how does **MANUS** measure up against these formidable competitors, and what does its emergence mean for the future of **AI-driven automation**?

The Competitive Landscape: Anthropic, OpenAI, and Google

- **Anthropic**, a relatively new player in the AI field, has focused heavily on **AI safety** and ensuring that its **AI models** are designed in a way that minimizes harmful behavior. Their models are known for being highly **conscious of ethical considerations** and are built with the intention of mitigating risks associated with **AI decision-making**.

Their **Claude** model, an advanced **conversational AI**, aims to create intelligent systems that align closely with human values. While **Claude** is not as generalized as **MANUS**, it offers a compelling alternative in the realm of AI systems that prioritize **ethical behavior**.

- **OpenAI**, the creator of the **GPT** series (including GPT-4 and its variants), has revolutionized the field of natural language processing. With its release of **ChatGPT**, OpenAI introduced a conversational agent that can perform tasks ranging from **writing** and **coding** to **problem-solving** and **content creation**. However, while OpenAI's models are highly capable, they remain **specialized**—great at a range of tasks but still constrained by a lack of **general intelligence**. GPT-4, for example, does not possess the **autonomous decision-making** capabilities that **MANUS** offers. **MANUS**'s **multi-agent architecture** and ability to work autonomously across a variety of tasks sets it apart from **OpenAI's** current offerings.

- **Google**, with its extensive research in artificial intelligence, has developed a number of powerful AI systems, including its **BERT** model for natural language understanding and the **Google Assistant**, a virtual assistant that competes with **Apple's Siri** and **Amazon's Alexa**. Google has also made significant strides in **AI-powered search** and **cloud computing**. However, like OpenAI, Google's AI models have yet to achieve the level of **general intelligence** demonstrated by **MANUS**. Google's AI, while immensely powerful and capable, still focuses heavily on **specialized functions** rather than the autonomous, **multi-faceted operations** seen in **MANUS**.

How MANUS Stacks Up

When comparing **MANUS** to these competitors, it's clear that the system is in a class of its own when it comes to **general AI agents**. The **multi-agent architecture** of MANUS allows it to handle a wide range of tasks simultaneously, collaborating with specialized sub-agents to produce comprehensive solutions. This is a major step beyond the capabilities of traditional AI systems like **Claude, ChatGPT**, or **Google Assistant**, which excel in narrow tasks but do not possess the autonomous, **cross-functional adaptability** of MANUS.

MANUS stands out because it is **not just a chatbot** or **personal assistant**—it is an **autonomous, multi-agent system** capable of handling complex tasks like **planning a trip**, **analyzing stock data**, **conducting real estate assessments**, and more. Its ability to **collaborate** with sub-agents on different components of a problem and execute complex multi-step processes without human intervention positions it as a next-generation **AI agent**. In terms of **market impact**, MANUS is making waves not only with its **powerful technology** but also through its **hype** and **limited availability**, driving a frenzy for **invitation codes**.

Where **MANUS** truly differentiates itself is in its ability to **automate tasks** that typically require significant **human input**. **OpenAI**'s **ChatGPT**, for instance, excels at understanding and generating text, but it requires human supervision when it comes to executing tasks like analyzing large data sets or making strategic decisions. In contrast, **MANUS** can handle these tasks with **greater autonomy**, thanks to its sophisticated architecture that includes not only a **centralized AI agent** but also a team of **sub-agents** dedicated to specific tasks.

The Future of AI Competition

Looking ahead, the **competition** in the AI space will only intensify. As **MANUS** and other **general AI systems** emerge, there will likely be a **shift** in the way businesses and individuals think about **AI**. Systems like **MANUS** have the potential to disrupt **traditional industries**, from **customer service** to **financial analysis**, by offering highly **automated, cross-functional solutions**.

As **AI adoption** continues to grow, predictions suggest that **by 2026**, we will see **widespread automation** across **enterprises**, with AI systems capable of taking over tasks that were once the domain of human workers. The question is no longer whether AI will impact our jobs or businesses—it's about **how quickly** and in **what ways** these changes will unfold. Will we see **AI agents** like **MANUS** become the **standard** for business operations, or will **specialized AI systems** maintain dominance in certain industries?

The next few years will be pivotal in determining how **AI competition** shapes the future of **general AI** and **automation**. With **MANUS** leading the charge, the future is undeniably bright for AI systems that can understand, collaborate, and execute tasks across multiple domains. But this **competition** is about more than just technological advancement—it's about **market adoption** and **public trust**. As more companies develop their own AI systems, consumers and businesses alike will need to carefully consider which AI agents can **truly deliver** the level of **autonomy**, **intelligence**, and **reliability** that they need.

In the end, the competition between **MANUS**, **Anthropic**, **OpenAI**, and **Google** will not only shape the future of **AI** but will also drive the **evolution of automation** in ways that we can't yet fully predict. The rise of **general AI agents** like **MANUS** signals a new era—one where machines are not just assistants but **autonomous agents** capable of transforming industries and redefining how we interact with technology. **MANUS**'s impact on the market is just the beginning, and its competitors will undoubtedly continue to innovate and refine their approaches to automation and AI-driven decision-making. The future is undoubtedly going to be shaped by this **competition**, and **AI** is poised to be the driving force behind the next industrial revolution.

Chapter 10: The Road Ahead – Will MANUS Become a Household Name?

A s **MONICA** continues to push the boundaries of what is possible with **general AI**, the company faces a set of scaling challenges that are inherent to the development of such a groundbreaking technology. The journey from **concept** to **real-world application** for a complex system like **MANUS** has not been without its hurdles. One of the most pressing concerns as the company looks to expand its reach is ensuring that the **infrastructure** behind **MANUS** is robust enough to handle the growing demand from users worldwide.

Scaling Challenges for Monica

The **scaling challenges** faced by **Monica** are multifaceted. For one, the **multi-agent architecture** that powers **MANUS** is incredibly complex. Each task that **MANUS** handles— whether it's **trip planning**, **data analysis**, or **strategic decision-making**—involves multiple **sub-agents** working together seamlessly. This requires a level of coordination and computational power that is difficult to maintain at scale, especially as the user base grows.

Furthermore, **Monica** has to contend with the **technical challenge** of continuously improving the **algorithms** and **AI models** that power **MANUS**. AI is an evolving field, and keeping **MANUS** on the cutting edge requires constant research and development. As demand increases, **Monica** needs to ensure that the system remains reliable, efficient, and capable of handling a variety of tasks without compromising on quality.

One of the significant scaling challenges comes in the form of **computational resources**. Running a system as sophisticated as **MANUS**, which involves **multiple agents** working on complex tasks, requires a massive amount of processing power. Ensuring that **MANUS** can operate efficiently at scale, without experiencing lag or bottlenecks, is no small feat. This challenge is compounded by the **need for secure infrastructure** to protect sensitive data and maintain user trust.

Additionally, as **MANUS** grows, there is the **challenge of user onboarding**. Making the system accessible to a wider audience requires creating an **intuitive interface** that can cater to both **tech-savvy users** and those who are not accustomed to interacting with AI. **Monica** will need to invest in building **training resources** and **support systems** to ensure that users can effectively utilize **MANUS** for a variety of tasks.

Future Accessibility of MANUS: Exclusive or Mass Market?

One of the most intriguing questions about the future of **MANUS** is whether it will remain an **exclusive tool** for a select group of users or if it will eventually become widely accessible to the masses. Currently, access to **MANUS** is **highly limited**, with **invitation codes** being the primary means of gaining entry. This exclusivity has fueled the **buzz** around the system, as demand has far exceeded supply. The limited availability has created a **frenzied market** for invitation codes, with people willing to pay **premium prices** just to get access to the platform.

However, **Monica** has made it clear that its long-term goal is to make **MANUS** available to a **broader audience**. The company is already laying the groundwork to scale its infrastructure and make the system more accessible as it continues to improve its underlying technology. There are several ways this could unfold:

- **Expanding User Access Gradually**: One option is for **Monica** to expand access to **MANUS** gradually, perhaps by allowing **premium users** or businesses first and then opening it up to the **general public** once the system can handle the load. This approach would allow the company to ensure that **MANUS** remains functional and reliable as it scales, while still tapping into the growing demand.
- **Commercial Licensing and Partnerships**: Another possibility is that **Monica** could form partnerships with businesses and organizations, offering them **licensed access** to **MANUS** for specific tasks. This could allow **MANUS** to reach a wider audience in industries like **tech**, **finance**, and **education**, while still maintaining some control over its accessibility. Over time, as the technology matures, **Monica** could open up the platform for broader use.

- **Public Launch and Freemium Model**: There's also the potential for **Monica** to release **MANUS** publicly as a **freemium service**, where anyone can access the basic functionality, but advanced features require a **subscription** or **one-time purchase**. This model has been effective for many software companies, as it allows users to experience the product without commitment while also generating revenue from those who need premium features.

In the long run, the future of **MANUS** is likely to follow the trajectory of other **AI-driven technologies**—starting out as an **exclusive tool** for those at the cutting edge, and eventually becoming a mainstream product that businesses and individuals alike use for a variety of tasks. However, **Monica** will need to carefully balance accessibility with the need to maintain a **high-quality user experience**. If the system becomes too widely available too quickly, it could lead to **technical issues** and an overall decline in the quality of service.

The **exclusivity** of **MANUS** may not last forever, but it has certainly created a **sense of urgency** and **anticipation** around the product. As more users gain access, we can expect the platform to evolve and expand, offering even more sophisticated features and capabilities. In time, **MANUS** could become a **ubiquitous tool** that reshapes the way we work, collaborate, and interact with **AI**—just as other groundbreaking technologies have done in the past.

Ultimately, the future of **MANUS** is a question of balance— how **Monica** manages scaling while maintaining the integrity of the platform and ensuring that **MANUS** can meet the needs of an increasingly demanding and diverse user base. Whether it remains an exclusive tool or becomes available to the masses, one thing is certain: **MANUS** will continue to play a pivotal role in shaping the future of **AI**.

As we look toward the future, the trajectory of **MANUS** over the next **5 to 10 years** promises to be nothing short of revolutionary. With its current capabilities already outpacing existing AI systems in terms of multitasking, collaboration, and autonomous decision-making, the evolution of **MANUS** will likely continue to push the boundaries of what artificial intelligence can achieve.

How MANUS Could Evolve Over the Next 5-10 Years

The next decade for **MANUS** could see several significant advancements, both in terms of its **technology** and its **applications**. Here's a glimpse into the potential evolution of **MANUS**:

1. **Improved Multi-Agent Collaboration** As **MANUS** continues to mature, its **multi-agent architecture** could become even more sophisticated. In the near future, **sub-agents** working within **MANUS** might operate even more independently, requiring less oversight and coordination from human users. These agents could specialize in **narrower tasks**, collaborating seamlessly on complex projects while learning and adapting in real time. With advancements in **reinforcement learning** and **autonomous problem-solving**, **MANUS** could evolve into an AI capable of executing highly intricate tasks

without human intervention.

2. **Contextual Understanding and Emotional Intelligence** One area where **MANUS** could see significant improvement is in its **understanding of human context**. In the future, we can expect **MANUS** to become increasingly attuned to emotional and social cues, allowing it to interact more naturally with human users. Imagine an AI that not only handles technical tasks like **data analysis** but also understands **human motivations**, emotions, and communication styles. This would elevate **MANUS** from being a tool to becoming a genuine **collaborator** in a variety of professional and personal environments.

3. **Enhanced Learning and Adaptation** As **MANUS** grows, it could achieve greater **autonomous learning capabilities**, allowing it to continuously **evolve and improve** without requiring constant updates from its creators. With more advanced machine learning algorithms, **MANUS** could learn from the data it interacts with, the decisions it makes, and the feedback it receives from its users, becoming even more intelligent and efficient as time goes on.

4. **Broader Industry Applications** Over the next decade, **MANUS** could expand into a wide variety of industries beyond **real estate**, **tech**, and **education**. As its capabilities grow, it might play a transformative role in **medicine**, **law**, **manufacturing**, and **government**. For example, in healthcare, **MANUS** could assist doctors with diagnosis, treatment recommendations, and even **personalized care plans** for patients. In law, it could automate contract review, legal research, and litigation strategy. The possibilities for **MANUS** to integrate into

diverse sectors are vast, and it's likely that we will see the system become an indispensable tool for businesses and professionals across the globe.

5. **Seamless Integration with Other Technologies** As AI systems like **MANUS** continue to evolve, we might see more **interconnected AI ecosystems** where **MANUS** works in tandem with other cutting-edge technologies like **quantum computing**, **blockchain**, and the **Internet of Things (IoT)**. This integration could create a hyper-connected world where MANUS helps facilitate everything from **smart cities** to **automated financial systems**, creating a level of synergy and efficiency never before seen.

6. **Ethical and Regulatory Developments** As **MANUS** becomes more ingrained in society, there will be increasing scrutiny around the ethical implications of its use. In the next 5-10 years, **MONICA** may need to address key issues like **data privacy**, **bias**, and **autonomous decision-making**. We can expect the rise of **global regulations** governing AI, ensuring that systems like **MANUS** are developed and used responsibly. This could lead to the creation of **ethical AI frameworks** that balance **innovation** with **human values**.

The Lasting Impact of MANUS on AI Technology and Human Productivity

Regardless of how **MANUS** evolves over the next decade, its lasting impact on both **AI technology** and **human productivity** will be profound. As we move toward a future where AI plays an even greater role in our daily lives, **MANUS** is likely to be at the forefront of this transformation.

1. **Revolutionizing Human Productivity** At its core, **MANUS** is designed to **automate complex tasks** and handle multi-step processes with ease. Over time, its widespread adoption could free up humans from the repetitive, time-consuming tasks that currently dominate the workplace. For businesses, this means more **efficiency** and **cost savings** as they can rely on **MANUS** to handle everything from **data analysis** to **strategic planning**. For individuals, it could lead to a more **balanced work-life dynamic**, as **MANUS** helps with personal tasks like **trip planning** or even **budget management**.

Imagine a future where an AI assistant not only schedules your meetings but also manages your finances, organizes your projects, writes reports, and even offers advice on career growth—all without you having to lift a finger. In this scenario, **MANUS** becomes an essential partner in maximizing **human potential**, enabling us to focus on more creative, strategic, and high-level thinking.

1. **The Democratization of Intelligence** One of the most exciting possibilities for **MANUS** is the potential for the **democratization of intelligence**. With its ability to analyze massive amounts of data, collaborate across multiple domains, and offer insights into complex systems, **MANUS** could put **advanced AI** into the hands of anyone who needs it—regardless of their technical expertise. This would **level the playing field** for small businesses, individuals, and even entire nations, providing them with access to tools that were once reserved for the tech elite.

2. **New Forms of Collaboration** The rise of **MANUS** could lead to new forms of collaboration between humans and AI. Over the next decade, we could see more **hybrid teams**, where AI systems like **MANUS** work alongside humans to tackle complex challenges. These collaborations could reshape industries, as AI takes on more of the heavy lifting while humans focus on creativity, emotional intelligence, and strategy. The **division of labor** between humans and machines will likely become more refined, resulting in a more **productive** and **innovative** workforce.

3. **Shaping Future AI Development MANUS** has the potential to **influence the entire field of AI development**. As one of the first true general AI agents, its success—or failure—could set the tone for future breakthroughs. **MANUS's** ability to integrate multiple **sub-agents** and perform a wide variety of tasks might become the **standard** for how AI systems are developed going forward. Other companies and developers will likely look to **MANUS** as a blueprint for their own innovations, pushing the entire field of AI toward greater **autonomy** and **collaboration**.

4. **A New Era of Human-AI Interaction** Ultimately, **MANUS** could usher in a new era of **human-AI interaction**, one where AI systems are not seen as mere tools but as collaborative partners in the pursuit of **greater understanding** and **innovation**. As **MANUS** evolves and becomes more deeply integrated into our lives, it could redefine how we approach **technology**, **work**, and **creativity**. The lasting impact of **MANUS** will not only be felt in the realm of **AI development** but also in the way **human beings interact** with machines, paving the

way for an **AI-powered future** where the possibilities are limitless.

In the next 5-10 years, **MANUS** is set to be a catalyst for some of the most significant transformations in the world of AI and productivity. The **breakthroughs** we are likely to witness will redefine how businesses operate, how we interact with technology, and what it means to truly collaborate with machines. The impact of **MANUS** will extend far beyond its initial capabilities, shaping the future of work, innovation, and human achievement.

Conclusion: The AI Revolution is Here – Are You Ready?

The world is on the brink of a monumental shift, one that will alter the way we work, interact, and understand technology itself. **MANUS**, as the first true **general AI agent**, is at the forefront of this revolution, showcasing the incredible potential of AI to transform every aspect of our lives. As we've explored throughout this journey, the rise of **MANUS** is more than just the emergence of a new technology—it's the dawn of a new era where **AI agents** will play an integral role in shaping business, society, and human progress.

The Potential Long-Term Impact of MANUS on Business, Technology, and Society

MANUS represents a paradigm shift in the way we perceive and use artificial intelligence. Its ability to **automate complex tasks**, **collaborate autonomously**, and **adapt to a wide range of industries** marks a turning point in **business operations** and **technological innovation**. The impact of **MANUS** will be felt across every sector, from **finance** to **healthcare**, and

real estate to **education**. As businesses adopt AI agents like **MANUS**, we will witness a complete overhaul of traditional workflows, unlocking new levels of **efficiency**, **productivity**, and **innovation**.

For society, **MANUS** holds the promise of democratizing access to cutting-edge technology. By breaking down barriers to entry, **MANUS** will enable individuals, businesses, and even governments to leverage the power of AI without requiring a deep understanding of complex coding or machine learning. The **economic landscape** will change as **MANUS** empowers more people to create, collaborate, and innovate, leading to a surge of **creativity** and **entrepreneurship** that was once unimaginable.

The Role of AI Agents in Shaping the Future of Work and Life

As we look toward the future, **AI agents** like **MANUS** will become more than just tools—they will be **partners**, collaborators, and even mentors. In the workplace, AI will no longer be viewed as an outsider that performs repetitive tasks; it will be seen as a **team member** that contributes to high-level decision-making, strategic planning, and creative problem-solving. The future of **work** will be a **cooperative environment**, where humans and AI systems work side by side to achieve goals that were previously unattainable.

On a broader scale, the integration of AI agents like **MANUS** into our daily lives will reshape how we live, communicate, and interact with the world. These systems will become more **intu-**

itive, **adaptive**, and **human-like**, making it easier for people to engage with technology in a more natural and fulfilling way. The **work-life balance** will shift, as AI systems like **MANUS** handle time-consuming tasks, allowing individuals to focus on more **meaningful** and **purposeful** activities. From managing personal schedules to analyzing complex data, the impact of AI will touch every corner of human existence, making our lives easier, more productive, and more connected.

How MANUS Fits into the Broader Picture of Technological Advancement

When we zoom out and consider the broader landscape of technological advancement, **MANUS** is part of a larger **movement** toward **autonomous systems**, **smart environments**, and **digital transformation**. It is not an isolated phenomenon, but rather a critical piece of a much bigger puzzle in the development of **Artificial General Intelligence (AGI)**, **machine learning**, and **automation**.

MANUS is a key player in the ongoing journey toward more sophisticated, **self-sufficient** AI systems—systems that can adapt, learn, and improve with minimal human intervention. As **MANUS** continues to evolve, it will pave the way for the next generation of **AI agents**, each more advanced and capable than the last. In many ways, **MANUS** is laying the groundwork for a future where **AI** is seamlessly integrated into every facet of human life, from personal tasks to complex enterprise solutions.

In the grand scheme of technological progress, **MANUS** represents the culmination of decades of research, development, and innovation in the field of artificial intelligence. It is a breakthrough that will be remembered as a defining moment in the history of **AI development**, just as the advent of the **internet**, **smartphones**, and **cloud computing** were.

Final Thoughts: The AI Revolution is Here—Are You Ready?

The **AI revolution** is no longer a distant concept—it's happening right now, and **MANUS** is leading the charge. As we stand on the precipice of this new age, it is crucial to understand the profound impact that **AI agents** will have on the way we live and work. **MANUS** is not just a technological marvel; it is a glimpse into a future where **AI** is a central force in shaping the world around us.

As we move forward, the key question remains: **Are you ready for the AI revolution?** Are we prepared to embrace a future where artificial intelligence is as integral to our daily lives as the internet or smartphones? The rise of **MANUS** signals the beginning of an exciting new era, one where **AI agents** will empower us to do more, be more, and achieve more than we ever thought possible.

In the end, **MANUS** is just the beginning. The future of AI is vast, and the possibilities are endless. The revolution is here, and we are just getting started.